MANU SCRIPTI

BEYOND BOOKS

NITISH SHARMA

Made with ♥ on the Notion Press Platform
www.notionpress.com

Contents

In Sanatan Dharma, Lord Ganesha is the first deity to be remembered before starting work. He is known for his curved trunk and magnificent body, which shines as brightly as a million suns. Oh, mighty Lord, please bless my work and remove any obstacles that may come my way.

Lord Ganesha is the Son of Devi Parvati and Mahadev Shiva. He is the most intelligent Deity among the Divine. People worship him because he is considered the remover of obstacles and brings prosperity to life. But when we look closely Bhagwan Ganesha depicts many hidden treasures of

Knowledge, that are beyond the understanding of a normal Human.

Now let us see what we know about Lord Ganesha: He has a Head of Elephant.

He is the first to be remembered before performing any ritual, Pooja, or auspicious work.
He uses a Mouse as his Vahana (Vehicle). He removes Obstacles.
He is the Husband of RIDHI(Wealth) and SIDHI (Intellect).

Once upon a time, Sage Devrishi Narad arrived on Mount Kailash with a Divine Mango that he had received from Lord Brahma. He presented it to Devi Parvati, saying that whoever consumed the mango would gain extraordinary qualities and powers. Being a loving mother, she wanted to divide the mango between her two sons: Lord Kartikeya (the elder) and Lord Ganesha (the younger). However, there was a condition attached to the mango – it could only be consumed by one person completely.

This led to a competition between the brothers, with rules stating that whoever completed the three rounds of the world first would be declared the winner and presented with the mango. Lord Kartikeya swiftly mounted his peacock and soared into the skies as the race began. Meanwhile, Lord Ganesha, who had no such Vahana (vehicle), thought his parents were his whole world. With his love for them, he started walking around them and completed three rounds.

Lord Ganesh was declared the winner of a contest due to his wisdom. He taught the world the importance of being grateful to one's parents. He is often depicted with a mouse as his companion, symbolizing that even small things can provide great knowledge if one has insight. He is the Husband of Wealth and Intellect, signifying that a wise person can remove obstacles in their path with the use of wealth and intellect. He has the head of an elephant, which represents someone who uses his/her intellect and wisdom to solve problems can work like an elephant in the jungle, overcoming any obstacle that stands in the way.

The reason Lord Ganesh is worshipped first is not entirely clear. However, the answer lies within a story that requires an understanding of the concept of Shivalya. When visiting a temple of Shiva, there is a water passage of Shiva lingam (jaleri) that one does not cross during Prakirma, which is the act of walking around the temple. This signifies that no one can bind the sacred energy of Lord Shiva and Parvati in the entire world. However, Lord Ganesh was the only one able to perform the Prakirma of both deities three times. This shows that he has the sharp insight to understand the cause and effect of the entire creation. Combining all these qualities makes him the God that teaches humans to be more intellectual and firmer while doing any activity for a good cause. This is why he is worshipped first in all the rituals, reminding humans to work with intelligence.

About The Author

Nitish Sharma's journey from childhood curiosity to his profound understanding of Sanatan Dharma is indeed intriguing.

Starting with his early fascination with mechanical toys and their inner workings, he developed a keen analytical mind. This curiosity eventually led him to pursue mechanical engineering, where he likely honed his systematic approach to understanding complex systems.

Later in life, Nitish Sharma's interest shifted to Sanatan Dharma, the ancient spiritual and philosophical tradition of India. He describes this as a profound tantra, indicating his belief that it holds deep secrets and insights into the nature of existence. His journey into understanding Sanatan Dharma was not merely academic but transformative, guided by what he perceives as direct spiritual experiences and visions.

In his book, Nitish Sharma presents a comprehensive exploration of Sanatan Dharma. He aims to unveil the intricate structure of Dharma, which he believes has been present but not fully understood by many. His approach combines both logical analysis and foundational insights, offering readers a pathway to comprehend the essence behind the rituals, beliefs, and the deeper workings of Dharma.

According to Sharma, grasping the essence of Sanatan Dharma has the potential to awaken individuals to their true purpose in life. It promises to reveal insights into the relationships between gods, their realms, and humans, as perceived through the lens of this ancient tradition.

Overall, Nitish Sharma's journey from mechanical toys to spiritual enlightenment through Sanatan Dharma showcases a unique perspective blending scientific curiosity with profound spiritual exploration. His book seeks to bridge the gap between intellectual understanding and spiritual awakening, inviting readers to delve deeper into the timeless wisdom of Dharma.

Introduction

Curiosity fuels our quest for knowledge, guiding us through the vast realms of understanding. It sparks a hunger to unravel the universe's mysteries, driving us to seek wisdom beyond what is known. With each question asked and each answer sought, curiosity leads us on a journey of self-discovery and enlightenment. When human limits are reached, imagination takes flight, transcending reality's constraints. It allows us to envision endless possibilities, from distant galaxies to the depths of consciousness. Let's embrace curiosity, nurture imagination, and embark on an exploration of the universe's wonders.

Now, imagine hovering ten feet above your room, observing its familiar details—the contours of your body, the space it occupies, and the surrounding objects.

"Wait, don't read further. Really imagine what I said, and then move on to the next paragraph."

As you hover above, observe your smallness in the vastness around you—the furniture, walls, and floor stretching out, highlighting the scale of your world. Reflect on your presence, the journey that brought you here, and the potential ahead. With each breath, feel connected to the universe, aware of your place within it. Embrace the power of imagination and envision endless possibilities.

Now, zoom out from your village, expanding your perspective. Witness the transition from streets to towns, districts, and states, revealing the interconnected web of civilization. Soar above your country, seeing its diversity and beauty. Zoom further to your continent, experiencing its cultures and landscapes. Finally, behold Earth, a fragile orb in space, and zoom out to see the cosmos. Feel awe and wonder, recognizing your smallness yet connection to the universe's fabric. Through this unity, glimpse a greater purpose beyond understanding.

People often focus on materialistic desires, but we can only eat a limited amount of food daily — about 1.5 kg for an adult, enough to sustain a 70 kg body. Now, let's return to reality. If I touch your toes and ask, "Is this you?" you will deny it, and continue denying it with each body part I touch. But when I touch the center of your chest and ask the same question, you will say yes.

This is because every element in this universe is trying to find the resting place for its existence, the center of gravity or equilibrium is where we feel most comfortable. Our brain creates an illusion of a vast dimensional plane, which we perceive as reality. In conclusion, our brain plays a game with us every day, and we are like a Pendulum, constantly seeking equilibrium in our lives. To come out of this illusion and be one with the universe is to know that we are nothing but a form of energy living through ever changing Human consciousness doing karma.

Humans are living in the golden era of pleasure, where every luxury is available with just a click. When we can grow green vegetables in deserts and apples in warm weather, every earthy element is available or can be delivered to our doorstep. It doesn't matter if the land where we live (Country) has the resources to produce it. It all depends on what we demand.

Well, speaking about demand, if I say our demand depends on our imagination, then I won't be wrong; after all, everything HUMANS do from morning till night is imagining.

For example, our body sends a signal to our brain that it is feeling uneasy due to the hot temperature, and all of a sudden, we have the urge to cool down our body temperature to feel at ease. For that purpose, we have an air conditioner. we turn it on and there we have it, a cold breeze of snowy mountain air blowing at our face right in the middle of a scorching summer afternoon.

All of the scenarios beg the question: even after having all kinds of luxuries, we won't find a single person on Earth who is using all these luxuries and still happy with his/her life, which is contradictory to the statement that we are living in the golden era of pleasures. So, there must be something wrong we might be doing. There must be some flaws lying in what reality is and what imagination is.

We as Humans have entered the Iron Age (Kali Yuga) where science and technology are providing every known gadget and solutions to problems in the form of equipment and data. Dharma is playing a negligible role in today's world. Since everything is being operated by Industrial Mindset every aspect of life on Earth has become the resource of either food or money to the Human.

The run for this empty race has turned Manushyas (Human) into Daitya (Deamon), where he has gone haywire, Even knowing the fact that whatever he has collected throughout his life will stay on Earth and nothing will go with him to the afterlife. This realization leads to the question of what he will be carrying to the next life; the answer is simple: Karmas.

Today's world has many religions that talk about Gods in their own ways and then there is Dharma originated from the land of Bharat, which talks about Bhagwan as well, but both have different essences to the working.

Religions talk about God in the sense that he is a Carpenter, which makes him control all the time and if you do not believe in their particular Gods, you will go to hell. There is no concept of karma in their core and all the teachings are directed towards the essence where you are either a slave or wrongdoer of God's kingdom and this human life is granted to you only to believe in them and it does not affect your core principles being wrong like killing animals or looting other people. You, as a believer of that particular God, have no other duty than to believe in him. Religions make people think that other people who do not believe in their particular Gods will go to hell, which seems to be putting in fear rather than liberating the person.

Contrary to this thought Sanatan Dharma's teachings are mainly directed towards the person reading the Dharma or trying to follow it. The whole structure stands on the principle of KARMA. There is a reaction that the person will face to every good deed or wrong action, making him aware of the energies in his body and the Gods sitting in Universe in the form of energy. Principals that, when applied to the life of any person, will get him out of illusion. To understand this TANTRA, we have to start from the very beginning of this coded Dharma, which is believed to be of no significance by the religions.

Dharma works in a way that liberates a person from the nonsense worries made up by the modern world. Activities that are being followed by today's humans as a part of their livelihood include working as a rat trapped in a cage, eating like a pig on a farm, and enjoying the fake euphoria of a materialistic world like Satan in hell. Doing activities that are harming the planet Earth for the unsatiable lust of Gadgets, KILLING animals for just the taste of tongue or just for fun, and destroying jungles to mine more and more resources for the sake of money. Contrary to this, Dharma teaches about what is most beneficial for humans and Mother Earth. It tells a human not to harm nature and to respect it in the form of God and if we look at the broad spectrum of Dharma, it is the best possible way to lead a life while living healthy by eating foods that do not harm the body in any sense and letting the nature thrive by building a place of worship that contains ponds and creating ecosystems that helps the nearby animals have food and water easily and readily available.

Dharma teaches a human how to offer food to animals, water the plants, and worship both of them as a part of spiritual activity which will give a person eternal peace and turn his abomination towards the outer world into a never-ending love story that benefits society, earth, and animals living around him. To understand the vast dimension of how this tantra works, we will have to start from the very beginning of the trinities and their wives coming into existence, unfolding the real meanings of the elements and their subparts affecting the Human life.

This is where this MANU SCRIPTI enters. Reading this will not open your eyes. Beware. It is directly and powerfully going to make you understand the dimensions that no other book could. You will see things happening right in front of your eyes.

Everything was clear and pristine and was present in front of you. But just because it is a human mentality to exploit resources and make them poisonous, the real meanings of the workings of NATURE, GODS, and HUMANS got lost.

This MANU SCRIPTI works in such a form that you will not have to decipher whether it's Fiction or Reality. All it took was 18 years of continuous experiences and meditation to come out of a fictitious world that we live in and see for myself what GOD is and compile all that in one book.

CHAPTER ONE

GENERAL BELIEF OF FOLLOWERS

In modern-day Bharat, people have very little time to decipher or to learn about the real Dharma. They get the Dharmic vibes only on special occasions or festivals that are celebrated across the Bharat.

So, people mainly follow or worship Indian Gods in the Pagan way of believing in the Entity, i.e., to go to the temple out of fear or to pray to Gods to get something.

The basic understanding of the complete Sanatan tantra has been lost. The most common Bhagwan that are being followed in Bharat are: SHIVA with PARVATI and GANESHA, RAM LAKSHMAN and SITA with Bhakt VEER HANUMAN, KRISHNA with RADHA, NARAYAN with LAKSHMI, MAA DURGA, MAA KALI and KARTIKEYA in SOUTH INDIA.

A battle is going on inside Dharma among the followers of SHIVA, VISHNU, and SHAKTI. The battle is not about who the bigger god is; the battle is of Ego that gets served by how fluent a person is in reciting the Verses of various religious scriptures.

This battle is not started by the normal people who come from villages; this is a war among people who live in cities or towns and they try to impose their superiority on others by glorifying their particular sect, as it gives them a feel of satisfaction that after attaining this much wealth, we are much closer to the meaning of GOD and we are superior to others as our sect people are considered more of strict followers of the rules described by some random GURU.

These types of mentalities are the real cause of DHARMA's losing its effectiveness in today's world, even in various Puranas, Bhagwan VISHNU, and Bhagwan SHIVA themselves have said many times: the people who will try to create a difference between both us will be offender to both of us.

So, the question arises: who is doing this separation?
It is Kali (the final yuga Deamon) himself; He is the one who took the form of different fake Gurus to divided Dharma into sects and make people fight with each other over the fake power that they attain after demeaning other Gods or Sects related to them.

When Kali the Demon was born, he was holding his tongue in one hand and his Penis in the other hand depicting the type of people that would be in his yuga. People will not have control over their speaking and their sexual desires will lead to an insatiable lust for power over other people. If we see today's humans, they are all behaving as if all they want to achieve is power over other beings or fellow humans and their sexual desires have become so absurd that Women do not feel safe in this era.

There is no control over how many sexual partners a person be it a Male or Female is having. It seems like lust has taken control over the minds of the people and they are living the life of an animal in a human's body.

CHAPTER TWO

BASICS OF SANATAN DHARMA

The piece of land where DHARMA originated was where people led a life of peace, tranquility, and sustainability where culture was so deeply rooted in the people. They had never named their set of beliefs or the set of rules into some particular word like religion, because no ego or hatred had to be served as a part of imposing their superiority on the people who didn't believe in their society, that land had a name that got changed many times.

ARYAVATA, currently known as Bharat, was invaded and looted many times by different looters, namely The Mughals, The Mongols, The Britishers, The Dutch, The Portuguese and many others. The only country in the world that has many names today, like Bharat, India, Hindustan, Aryavarta, Jambudweep, Tenjiku, Al-hind and many more.

These names are the outcome of the oppression and ruling of different dynasties on this piece of land and because of so many Abrahamic religious oppressors, the real sense of Dharma got lost in the time laps as those religions continuously tried to destroy the dharma and bring people to their Religion for the daily activities and loot the resources permanently from this land.

Unable to convert the people of Bharat to their religions, they started destroying the religious scriptures and GURUKULS (schools) of ancient Bharat.

Attackers like Bakhtiyar Khilji first **DESTROYED NALANDA UNIVERSITY** in 1200 CE, which had ancient scriptures. After that, the Britishers did damage to the teachings of dharma by closing Gurukuls and making people feel **INFERIOR** about their language and culture, they declared that ancient scriptures like RAMAYANA, GEETA and MAHABHARATA were **MYTHOLOGIES** and till today, it is being taught in schools about Indian scriptures as **MYTH.**

Due to the poverty and hunger, people became desperate to get jobs and it became difficult for Dharmic teachings to exist in the Industrial revolution as INDIA found it easy to provide cheap labour, and earn money which was only possible through Schooling in English Medium for ongoing Industrial revolution. Slowly and steadily, SANSKRIT lost its roots and people got uprooted from a real sense of DHARMA. However, the log of wood always floats in water after the pressure is removed. So, the basic teachings remained.

Based on the scriptures, there are 3 main gods (TRIDEV), 33 KOTI Devtas, 4 VEDAS, 18 PURAN, 12 SHASTRAS, 4 YUGAS and 7 SAGES in Sanatan Dharma. Believers of Sanatan Dharma in today's world simply go to the temples designated to either Tridev or their specific Devtas. Veds and Purans are rarely read daily by followers. People just pray to GOD and indulge in their social life. Those who call themselves devotees most of the time are doing it in a SHOWOFF manner. The real sense of DHARMA is not being understood thus leading to a lot of confusion being portrayed and transferred to the next generation.

The basic principles of Sanatan Dharma stand on four pillars DHARMA, ARTH, KAM and MOKSHA. There are 7 main characters around which the whole game is being played: Gods, Humans, Atma, Devtas, Daityas, Animals and Nature. Gods are the creator of this world. Humans, Devtas, Daityas, Animals and Nature are their creations. Devtas and Daityas fight for the realms. Atma is the real essence of God that is affected by the body's Karma in Human form and if karma is bad, then Atma is given animal body.

According to the body that Atma receives, it gets knowledge about the food and the working of its limbs. All the animals were granted lower Chetna (Consciousness) in terms of GOD, LIFE and PURPOSE of that body so that the working of nature should not stop. And since the war had to be fought by humans, they were granted all the knowledge related to its soul, its Purpose, about Gods and all kinds of tantras that could help him define life in meaningful ways. To make humans more conscious, he was granted different emotions such as love, Kama and moksha. All those emotions were present in other animals except

MOKSHA (NIRVANA) which, when known, will kick start the journey of soul towards Devtas and Bhagwan (GODS). To balance things out and make it fair for Daitya's, emotions like jealousy, hatred, anxiety, fear and anger. All the positive and negative emotions were instilled in atma as a soft copy which, when triggered, will lead to Karma being initiated.

MANDIR, AND TILAK

In essence, place of worship stands as timeless monuments to humanity's eternal quest for meaning and transcendence. They intrigue seekers to embark on a journey of self-discovery, inviting them to unlock the doors of their minds and explore the boundless realms of the spirit. For that purpose, humans created Temples and in

Bharat they created Mandir. While in other religions Temples were created to gather people and give them the message of their particular GODS contrary to that in Sanatan Dharma MANDIRS were created at places where there was least population density serving as a place to feel the energy of supreme through solitude.

Mandirs were places where people could go and do dhyana(meditate).

The whole structure of Mandir was designed in such manner that the person who enters it automatically starts getting detached from the outer world and its nonsense worries. After all, if we break the word Mandir it comes up to the meaning MAN (mind) Dar(door), So it is the gateway of our mind which allows us to go beyond our MIND by controlling the continuous demands of our Brain.

But if we see today's world People are Going in groups to these holy places like Picnic spot and asking for the materialistic desires which in a sense is ironical. People stand in front of the Vigrah and start asking for their problems not knowing that Supreme energies are putting you in problems to understand the simple fact about life that everything is going to end when you die. And before you die you must awaken your Chetna to a level that you start doing good Karmas and refrain from nature harming activities.

After offering water or flowers or anything to the deity people place a tilak on their Forehead and walk out of temple. Most of the people do not understand the real meaning of tilak, they think of it as an identity sign. Well, the real meaning behind a tilak is to activate your pineal gland easily. When you apply a tilak it is wet, be it Chandan or Kumkum or saffron or Haldi or any kind. After applying tilak when you sit in the temple quietly in Dhyana mudra, the place where tilak is applied starts drying and during this process, the skin under tilak starts getting concentrated which helps a Sadhak to do Dhyana very easily.

In essence, Mandirs stand as timeless monuments to humanity's eternal quest for meaning and transcendence. They beckon seekers to embark on a journey of self-discovery, inviting them to unlock the doors of their minds and explore the boundless realms of the spirit.

CHAPTER THREE

TRINITIES

The base structure of Sanatan Dharma stands on Trinities out of which the whole world appeared. There are three male Gods:

- BRAHMA
- VISHNU
- SHIVA

And three female goddesses are their wives, respectively:

- SARASWATI
- LAKSHMI
- PARVATI

The working of Male Trinities, as per modern-day is that BHRAHMA is the CREATOR, He creates the worlds and the organisms. VISHNU takes care of the whole creation. SHIVA is considered as the destroyer of the world. The working of all Female Trinities, as per modern-day perception, is that SARASWATI provides Knowledge,

LAKSHMI provides Wealth and PARVATI is in the form of NATURE.

This is what is being written in Vedas and Puranas, but the real essence of it is coded and when we decode, we come to know about PARAMATMA. But before knowing PARMATMA we need to understand what Trinities do or who they really are and why they are so important in Sanatan Dharma.

If we look at the basic structure of any organism, be it amphibian, aquatic or Terrestrial, there are three main functions that every organism has:

- Taking decisions from the brain
- Eating food nourishes the body and
- Procreating and passing the DNA to the next generation.

Now, when we look at the Tridev, all three are depicted in different stories that tell the same functions that are the basic structure of the organism.

There is a story of Brahma, Vishnu, and Mahesh (Shiva) about the positioning of Brahma and the amputation of his fifth head by Lord Shiva that is described in SHIV PURAN. Once Lord Vishnu was lying on his Seshnag and Brahma came to his Abode. Vishnu welcomed Brahma while lying on his bed, this made Brahma angry and he started saying Vishnu this is how you Treat your elders, are these your manners? Vishnu replied with words saying Oh Brahma you sit on the top of lotus that originates from my navel and you think you are older than me.

A verbal fight began, and all of a sudden, a long cylindrical structure stood between them. Both got stupefied; what in the world is this? The top end was way beyond clouds and was not visible to the naked eye. Mesmerized by the length of the structure, both decided to resolve the issue by finding the end of the structure and whoever reaches the end of this structure first will be the superior one. Vishnu took the form of a boar and started digging the Earth. He went to find its origin, and Brahma sat on his swan and took flight to find the top of the structure. It was the first Shiv lingam that appeared in front of them. After searching a lot, Vishnu returned, considering his defeat as he could not find the bottom. As Brahma was also unable to find the top, he thought of a lie and brought a KETKI flower with him back to vouchsafe for his lie that he found this flower on the top of the Lingam. As the flower vouched in favor of Brahma, Lord Vishnu bowed to Brahma considering him as superior. Watching this lie, Lord Shiva got furious and sent Kal Bhairav to cut Brahma's top-looking head. He cursed Brahma not to be worshipped by anyone and as the flower was part of his lie, Lord Shiva banished Ketki flower to be offered to him in any pooja.

This story tells us about Brahma's position, how many heads he has, and the role of Lord Shiva and Vishnu. Brahma has four heads and he is the creator of lies and illusions. Brahma is the brain part of any organism and he sits on the lotus that originated from the navel of Lord Vishnu. If we look at the body of a human, we see that he has four sensory organs on his face, viz. EYES, EARS, NOSE, TONGUE and fifth head, which is the ability to understand what is right and wrong that gets disconnected when a person is sexually aroused. Hence Brahma has Five

Heads. It is the brain that creates different dimensions through these sensory organs, and it sits on top of the spinal cord, which starts right from the back of the navel.

Lord Vishnu is said to be the nourisher of the world. Lord Vishnu's depiction is the same as that of the digestive system. Your stomach is lying on the intestines in the form of serpentine, just as the Lord Vishnu is lying on the Shesh nag. That is why Lord Vishnu is linked with SATVIK food. Devotees of Lord Vishnu are instructed to eat only Satvik food as it is good for the stomach.

Now Lord Shiva is considered the Destroyer of this world from where this depiction arrives. Maybe people were trying to fit these Tridev into the word God (Generator Operator and Destroyer). But in reality, Lord Shiva is said to be MAHAKAAL, which means beyond TIME not the destroyer. Even though people know, it is Lord Vishnu (Dash avatar) who ends the Yuga every time, they are just misinterpreting Lord Shiva as the destroyer of the world. Yet there is a name associated with him that is PASHUPATINATH (Father of all Animals) so how can he be the destroyer?

Shiva is the only God that is depicted in the form of ARDHNARESHWAR, which is the combination of SHIVA and PARVATI; the only God who has a son and a daughter born by consummating the marriage. Also, when we go to any Shiva temple, there is a lingam and yoni that is being worshipped, but people are people who want to cover everything up to make everything a mystery. Shiva lingam is worshipped as a symbol, without this part there is no essence to life. Moreover, life ends if there is no regeneration.

There is a story that is related to the formation of VIRYA (SPERM) linked with SHIVA. When Lord Shiva swallowed Devrishi Ushanas because he tried to rob Kubera of his wealth. Lord Shiva became angry at his act and swallowed Devrishi Ushana. During his stay in the stomach of lord Shiva, he learned about mritsanjivni after a long period he became very uncomfortable in that position and started praying to Lord Shiva. After praying for thousands of years, Lord Shiva allowed him to come out in the form of Shukranu(sperm). Thus, he was given the name of Shukracharya. This story depicts the role of Shiva.

It is the most sacred part that allows life to happen. It is the only part in any organism's body that differs MALE from FEMALE, as all other body parts are the same in both bodies. No matter the animal or plant, every living organism has Shiva and Shakti, which allows nature to regenerate. And we bow down to this mystery of the intertwined concept of creation from simple elements to a living organism.

Sanatan Dharma portrays the three main functions of the body as sacred. It celebrates the way our bodies work, helping us understand life better and connecting us to the divine using it as an instrument. It also believes that this divine presence exists not just in humans but in all living things. It's like a child being amazed by toys that move on their own and clapping for them.

CHAPTER FOUR

PARAMATMA

There is a continuous war going on between Good and Bad on this Earth. This war is not new to this world. It all started when supreme energies came into existence. The universe consisted of two properties: Stillness and Momentum.

The stillness took the form of SHIVA and the momentum took the form of SHAKTI. These two further started dividing themselves into BHRAHMA AND VISHNU by SHIVA and SHAKTI gave rise to SARASWATI and LAKSHMI. Each form had a different functionality to maintain the balance of energy. All six combined created a functional Supreme being known to humans as PARAMATMA.

PARMATMA:- Combination of male and female TRINITIES

BRAHMA: The creator of illusions and Realms.

SARASWATI: The knowledge giver and illusion Remover

BODY

VISHNU: The preserver as well as the destroyers of worlds.

LAKSHMI: Wife of VISHNU The wealth giver

BRAIN

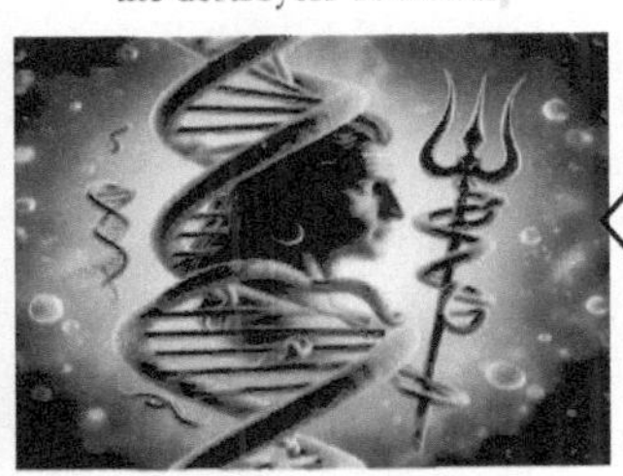

SHIVA– The holder of information about origin

SHAKTI: Birth giver to the information of Shiva

ORIGIN

CHAPTER FIVE

FORMATION OF DEVTAS, DAITYAS, AND HUMANS

With all six (Female and Male Trinities) coming into existence from infinity, it was time to create finite, as there formed different realms and Lokas that were standing still, A never-ending silence which was making all three Goddess restless as their purpose to provide knowledge, provide wealth, and regenerate was not getting fulfilled.

So, all six gathered and gave an Ansh (Portion) of all their divinity and created the normal human beings Manu (male) and Shatrupa (female) who procreated to have children and populated Earth. These Humans had all the Devtas and Daityas situated in the body.

The Seven sages that were disciples of Lord Shiva also came out of all six gods were called Sapt Rishis who meditated on Lord Shiva and made Manushyas (Humans) aware of the workings of the human body as well as the society.

The names of these Sages are:

1. ANGIRAS
2. ATTRI
3. KRATU
4. MARICHI
5. PULAHA
6. PULATSYA
7. VASISHTHA

Rishi Marichi married the daughter of Manu and Shatrupa, named Kala, to whom Rishi Kashyap was born.

DAKSH (Prajapati) was also born by the Ansh of six gods and married the daughter of Manu and Shatarupa named Prasuti, who gave birth to Diti and Aditi, along with 14 other siblings.

Rishi Kashyap married DITI and ADITI had children called Daityas (Born to Diti) and Adityas or Devtas (Born to Aditi), who started fighting for Lokas.

The sons of Diti were the embodiment of negative energy that was formed when Tridev came into existence, and it needed a physical form to exist. The same is true of Devtas, which were the embodiment of all positive energies.

Many other beings came into existence with these marriages, e.g., Gandharvas (the music players in Indralok), Apsaras (entertainers who danced in the heavenly realm of Indra on the music created by Gandharvas). Yakshas were the mystical creatures who dwelt in forests and guarded the jungles.

VISHVAKARMA, the lord of creative arts, was the incarnation of Lord Shiva himself, who created chariots and different mansions for Devtas.

Animals were made by all six to start the working of the Earth. They were created to work autonomously and have less Chetna (consciousness) than human beings.

So, everything we see on Earth today was created by the Trinities, laying the basic foundation for how our planet works. In various scriptures, Earth is also known as Bhur Loka or Mrityu Loka.

CHAPTER SIX

33 TYPES OF DEVTAS DECIPHERED

In Sanatan Dharma all Gods are further described into 33 types of Deities that are classified to 8 VASUS + 12 ADITYAS + 11 RUDRAS + 1 INDRA + 1 PRAJAPATI.

<u>8 VASUS</u>: The 8 Vasus are the elements that can be either felt or seen by the human.
Names of these gods are:

1. DYAUS - SKY
2. PRITHVI - EARTH
3. VAYU - AIR
4. AGNI - FIRE
5. NAKSHATRA - 27 CONSTELLATIONS
6. VARUN - WATER
7. SURYA - SUN
8. CHANDRAMA - MOON

<u>12 ADITYA</u>: The 12 ADITYA are the sons of Aditi, who are deities of different aspects of the position of SUN.
Names of these Deities are:

1. DHATA
2. ARYAMAN
3. MITRA
4. VARUNA
5. INDRA
6. VIVASVAN
7. TVASHTHA
8. VISHNU
9. AMSHUMAN
10. BHAGA
11. PSUHYA
12. PRAJANYA

<u>11 RUDRAS</u>: The 11 Rudra are forms of Lord Shiva. Also, the 11 bodily systems that act as the working mechanisms of the human body.
Names of these Deities are:

1. KAPALI
2. PINGALA
3. BHIMA
4. VIRUPAKSA
5. VILOHITA
6. AJAPADA
7. AHIRABRADHYA
8. SHASTA
9. SHAMBHU
10. CHANDA
11. BHAVA

<u>1 INDRA</u>: The controller of Inder Loka and king of all deities other than trinities.

<u>1 PRAJAPATI</u>: Prajapati is the controller of social activities.

Now, it is hard for a normal person to understand why to worship these gods as there seems no relevance in these deities, which is somewhat palpable, but if we decode it further, we understand the real meanings of 33 Koti of Devtas that are directly linked to the humans and a wide understanding about these deities.

Now when we examine closely all these Devtas are part of human body or affecting human body in different aspects of life as everything that is present in Sanatan Dharma texts is related to human body itself. Be it YOG, TANTRA, MANTRA, or YANTRA every mechanism is designed to use the human body as a tool to contact the PARAMATMA. Understanding these fact makes it easier to decipher that:

<u>1 INDRA-</u> Indra is depicted as holding a vajra made out of rishi Dadhich's skeleton, depicting that Indra controls the human body, and whenever Daityas attacks Indra's Loka starts trembling like whenever a human does bad deeds, his indri (Panch tattvas) get affected. also, in every story, whenever some rishi or normal human started doing meditation, the throne of Indra started trembling, which is a clear depiction that whenever a human starts meditation, his sensations start attacking him, making him remember more about tasty foods or sensual pleasures and other worldly pleasures so that the person gets distracted and do not do this activity. so, Indra is the controller of the Panch

tattvas that constitutes to form the human body.

1 PRAJAPATI- Daksh was the first Prajapati to knit the world in social activities and create a society out of Rishis and Manushyas. All of his story is centered on Yagya or HAVAN. So, the Yagya or Havan the purifier of the atmosphere as well as the ATMA of a Manushya.

8 VASUS: The 8 Vasus are the elements that impact directly on the human. And can be either felt or seen by humans. Names of these gods are:

1. Dyaus Sky
2. Prithvi Earth
3. Vayu Air
4. Agni Fire
5. Nakshatra (27 Constellations)
6. Varun Water
7. Surya Sun
8. Chandrama Moon

12 Aditya = The Sun enters 12 seasons around the year that affect the HUMAN

Names	Ruling Month	Lunar Month
1) Dhata	March-April	Chaitra
2) Aryaman	April-May	Vaishakha
3) Mitra	May-June	Jyeshtha
4) Varuna	June- July	Ashadha
5) Indra	July- August	Sharavana
6) Vivasvan	August- September	Bhadrapada
7) Tvashtha	September-October	Ashvina
8) Vishnu	October-November	Kartika
9) Amshuman	November-December	Margashirsha
10) Bhaga	December- January	Pausha
11) Psuhya	January- February	Magha
12) Parjanaya	February- March	Phalguna

<u>11 RUDRAS</u>: The 11 RUDRAS represent the 11 active body systems that work selflessly without any effort and constitute the basic human structure:

- CIRCULATORY SYSTEM
- LYMPHATIC SYSTEM
- RESPIRATORY SYSTEM
- INTEGUMENTARY SYSTEM
- ENDOCRINE SYSTEM
- GASTROINTESTINAL SYSTEM
- URINARY SYSTEM
- MUSCULOSKELETAL SYSTEM
- NERVOUS SYSTEM
- REPRODUCTIVE SYSTEM
- IMMUNE SYSTEM

CHAPTER SEVEN

ANOTOMY

After creating plants, animals, and other elements to support life on earth, it was now time to program the whole structure so that could work automatically. the war had to be fought by Devtas and Daityas without the interference of gods and their powers.

Three basic formats of life were created:

- Non-moving = JAD
- Moving without consciousness = ACHETAN
- Conscious = SACHETAN

JAD = All life forms that remain STILL throughout their lives are called 'Jad.' They carry the purest and oldest soul within them. When these souls transcend, they become elements like air, water, or earth. The purpose of Jad life forms is to provide food, purify the environment, and bring calmness to both SACHETAN (conscious) and ACHETAN (unconscious) Atma. They don't expect anything in return for their services on Earth. The highest atma attain this status after performing the finest deeds during their Sachetan life. Jad life forms include plants, shrubs, and trees.

ACHATEN= Earth needs an army of workers to help regenerate the environment. This can only happen through the continuous movement of resources among the 84 lakh species of non-conscious beings. These beings were created to adapt to specific environments, with Brahma, Vishnu, and Mahesh (representing creation, preservation, and regeneration) present within them. The Atma progress from lower to higher levels of consciousness within their bodies. They will perform their duties according to their body type, serving both purification and service to the Earth. The only difference between SACHETAN (conscious) and ACHETAN (unconscious) beings is that Achetan cannot understand the concept of God and Karma. Achetan life forms include all creatures except humans.

SACHETAN = The only form of life that has a complete understanding of others as well as of oneself is the human being. This is because humans can speak, read, write, and express their feelings, making them the exact representation of God Himself. Within them, the divine essence of Brahma activates all senses. Humans serve as tools for both gods and demons to fight the wars at the end of cosmic cycles. They are the only ones who fully comprehend and observe societal structures. Since humans are influenced by both gods and demons, they are given complete information about them, as well as the universe, in the form of coded messages. After experiencing all 84 lakh species of life on Earth, the soul is allowed to take a human birth. Depending on the karma performed in the conscious body, the soul will either be reborn as human, revert to an animal form, be born as non-conscious (Jad) life, or directly attain liberation (Parmatma).

Sachetan beings are the only ones capable of creating a society and establishing rules to fulfil various duties throughout their lives. To do so, they need to understand the concepts of KARMA and duty (KARTAVYA). Both Karma and Kartavya serve as stepping stones for the soul to attain liberation (moksha), which is the ultimate goal of being human. The duties performed by individuals are called DHARMA, while actions that go against nature or harm others are termed ADHARMA. By fulfilling their duties, individuals gain wealth (ARTH), and to continue the cycle of life, they must also understand the concept of desire (KAM). These principles collectively form the foundation of being human and determine the soul's subsequent births.

CHAPTER EIGHT

HUMAN ASTRAL BODY

The humans are divided into 4 types of Elements as per the birth of a child in different RASHI. All 4 Element are encapsulated in 5th Element that is AKASH Tatva. These elements are controlled by different Devtas.

These four elements are Fire, Water, Earth and Air.

These 4 elements are controlled by the Rashi (ZODIACS) for example:

- FIRE – ARIES, LEO, SAGITTARIUS
- WATER – CANCER, SCORPIO, PISCES
- EARTH – TAURUS, VIRGO, CAPRICORN
- AIR – GEMINI, LIBRA, AQUARIUS

The illustration of a birth chart is given below:

2. TAURUS
EARTH
ARTH

1.
ARIES
FIRE
DHARMA
(Lagna)

12. PISCES
WATER
MOKSHA

3.
GEMENI
AIR
KAM

11.
ACQUARIOUS
AIR
KAM

4.
CANCER
WATER
MOKSHA

10.
CAPRICORN
EARTH
ARTH

5.
LEO
FIRE
DHARMA

7.
LIBRA
AIR
KAM

9.
SAGITTARIOUS
FIRE
DHARMA

VIRGO
6. EARTH
ARTH

8.
SCORPIO
WATER
MOKSHA

The Rashi lord will be decided by the position of the moon in the BIRTH CHART of the person and his Previous life KARMAS will decide the placements of different planets sitting in 12 different HOUSES of the BIRTH CHART.

The numbers written in the house are the number of Rashis and the first house will always be considered LAGNA house and any number could be written in the first house as per the movement of planets during the birth of a human.

These houses will be acquired by 7 planets and 2 shadows. 7 PLANETs:

1.   MERCURY: The lord of WISDOM
2.   VENUS: The lord of LUXURIES

3. MARS: The lord of WAR.
4. SUN: The lord of FAME.
5. JUPITER: The lord of KNOWLEDGE.
6. SATURN: The lord of KARMA.
7. MOON: The lord of MIND.

2 SHADOWs:

1. RAHU: The one who has only a Head and has no Body and acts as a PROBLEM GIVER.
2. KETU: The one who has only a body but no Head and acts as a PROBLEM GIVER.

All the HOUSES have four different aspects as per SHASTRA:

<u>DHARMA</u>: This represents the spiritual nature of the 1st, 5th and 9th HOUSE representing the duties for Mother Earth as well as society.

<u>ARTH</u>: This represents the 2nd, 6th and 10th house of attaining wealth and a luxurious life by remaining within the boundaries of Dharma.

<u>KAM</u>: This represents the 3rd, 7th and 11th HOUSE and the consumption of sensual activities by remaining within the boundaries of Dharma.

<u>MOKSHA</u>: This represents the attainment of NIRVANA(Moksha) during HUMAN life by performing Dharmic activities, which is represented by the 4th, 8th, and 12th HOUSE.

The lords of deities as per Vedic shastras of different RASHI (zodiac) are:

- ARIES, SCORPIO: MARS

- TAURUS, LIBRA: VENUS
- GEMINI, VIRGO: MERCURY
- CANCER: MOON
- LEO: SUN
- SAGITTARIUS, PISCES: JUPITER
- CAPRICORN, ACQUARIUS: SATURN

All the planets sitting in different zodiacs and different houses give different types of information about the PAST, PRESENT, AND FUTURE of a human being, and using this information, a person can determine the type of karma he needs to do in the present life. This chart can make a human aware of upcoming dangers, tell if any witchcraft or sorcery has been done to him, and help him find the solution as per the planets. This is the ability that VEDAS provides to humans in the form of blessings on the physical as well as mental levels. This information will be given to humans as SAMUDRIKA SHASTRA.

CHAPTER NINE

14 LOKAS

14 Lokas or realms were created in which Atma transcends, that are mentioned in Rigveda and different puranas. these consist of 3 main Lokas, which are conceived as main destinations as per the karma of the atma.

Swarg Loka, Bhur Loka and Narak Loka.

Swarg Loka (Heavens) consists of 6 Lokas above Bhur Loka, where Bhur Loka is planet earth: the physical realm where karma is done by Atma, and Narak Lokas (Hell)consists of 7 Lokas below the Bhur Loka.

Sanatan Dharma describes these Lokas as places where Atma is set to observe the consequences of the karma done by the human being in the lifetime and after death. At the same time in Garud purana, it is mentioned in chapter 16 that all these Lokas are present in the human body.

When observed, it can be easily deciphered that it is the consciousness of the human brain that travels through these Lokas during the lifetime of an Atma and Good karmas lead to the attainment of Swarg Lokas of euphoria and Bad karmas push the atma to the Nark Lokas of suffering.

At the time of death, wherever the consciousness of atma is residing out of three Lokas, i.e., Swarg Loka Bhur Loka or Nark Loka determines whether the atma will be born as human or animal or if the consciousness has reached Swarg Loka, it will attain moksha.

<u>UPPER LOKAS:</u>

1. Satya Loka (Crown Chakra – Sahasrara) – Pure consciousness, connection with the divine.
2. Tapa Loka (Third Eye Chakra – Ajna) – Intuition and spiritual insight.
3. Jana Loka (Throat Chakra – Vishuddha) –Communication and creativity.
4. Mahar Loka (Heart Chakra – Anahata) – Love and compassion.
5. Svar Loka (Solar Plexus Chakra – Manipura) – Personal power and self-confidence.
6. Bhuvar Loka (Sacral Chakra – Svadhishthana) – Pleasure and sensuality.
7. Bhur Loka (Root Chakra – Muladhara) – Survival and grounding.

<u>LOWER LOKAS:</u>

8. Atala (Fear and lust-HIPS) – Fear Lust, Promiscuity.
9. Vitala (Rage and hate-Thighs) – Anger, Resentment.
10. Sutala (Jealousy-knees) – Jealousy, Covetousness.
11. Talatala (Confusion and Maya-Calves)-Greed, Deceit.
12. Mahatala (Lack of conscience-Knees).

13.   Rasatala (Selfishness-Over foot).

14.   Patala (Murderous instincts-Under foot).

<u>SEVENSAGES</u>

The SEVEN SAGES depict the Seven KUNDLINI chakras of the Human Body, which, when awakened by any human being through Dhyana and Yog, will lead to the opening of the SAHASRARA CHAKRA and will result in giving him information about his life purpose and will make that human stand among DEVTAS.

The name of these SEVEN CHAKRAS ARE

CHAPTER TEN

NADI

There are channels of energy in the human body that start from the nose and end at the base of the spinal cord, these channels are three in number. the names of these channels are Ida, Pingla and Shushmina.

<u>PINGLA:</u> starts with the right nostril and causes warmth in the body. this Nadi is associated with the energy of the sun. the purpose of this Nadi is to balance the bodily temperature, raise the blood pressure, and continue the practice of controlling the pingla Nadi helps a person to sit in Dhayan mudra for a longer period called Samadhi where he can control the various bodily functions just by breathing through the right nostril on demand in cold weathers.

<u>EDA:</u> starts with the left nostril and lowers the temperature of the body when continuous breathing is done through the left nostril. this Nadi is associated with the moon. The purpose of this Nadi is to help a person lower blood pressure and cool down the body in warm weather while doing the Dhyan mudra for a longer period, which is called Samadhi.

<u>SHUSHMINA:</u> when both the Nadi: Eda and Pingla are in control of a meditating person by doing Yog Sadhna, he can sit for longer times in Dhyan mudra and without moving an inch, he can control the bodily functions to feel at ease. the shushmina starts rising from Mooladhara (root chakra) till the Sahasrara (crown chakra). this led him to connect to the Parmatma and feel their presence. this will further lead to the clearing of thoughts, doing activities that are necessary for survival, and attaining the nirvana(moksha) stage. All of the information about the Yog and how to perform various body exercises will be given to humans in the Yog shastra.

Doing YOGA helps a person balance the energies inside his body, lead a happy and meaningful life by continuing practice that will give him knowledge about how to reach Paramatma by channeling his body as equipment to talk to Bhagwan.

CHAPTER ELEVEN

KARTAVYA & KARMA

KARTAVYA

The duty performed by an individual to provide sustenance for their family, ensuring they have food, clothing, and shelter, is considered kartavya. This responsibility is further categorized based on the Varna (social class) chosen by the individual after completing their education in a gurukul. In such schools, every student is taught a comprehensive curriculum covering various aspects of life by the age of 25. This education includes subjects such as Astras (weapons), shastras (scriptures), Vedas (ancient texts), culinary arts, mathematics, sciences, and more. After acquiring this knowledge and receiving specialized training in their chosen field, individuals are prepared to select their varna based on their aptitudes and inclinations.

Four varnas were specified for the accurate working of humans to create and operate a mechanism called society, which were:

1. **BRAHMINS:** those who spend their lifetime attaining the work of gods using their keen insight, and receive their earnings from society in the form of Bheeksha or alms. they were basically scientists who knew about Brahm and helped kings as well as the poor to bring meaning to their lives as per society and lead them to moksha. Pandits came under brahmins who kept records of spiritual texts, operated gurukuls and taught various subjects to students.
   NOTE: A BRAHMIN COULD BE BORN IN ANY VARNA FAMILY.

2. **KSHATRIYA:** Those who were fearless and ready to defend their society from foreign attacks on dharma at the cost of their life, as well as to maintain a balance by not letting any unlawful act occur in society. basically, they were trained in gurukuls after various tests taken by the GURUS, a fearless, impartial and insightful person was selected by the Brahmins to operate the kingdom. no bloodline was to be forced, as nepotism would only lead to misuse of the IMMENSE power that came with the royalty. A kshatriya will earn the livelihood of his family through taxes paid by the society.
   NOTE: A KSHATRIYA COULD BE BORN IN ANY VARNA FAMILY.

3. **VAISHYA:** Those who did business either in their village or in cities and were the carriers of goods from one place to another so that the artefacts produced in one kingdom could reach another kingdom were called

Vaishyas. Most of the trades were barter trade among the common people of villages and when moving from one place to another, Vaishyas could trade the grains with the king's palace in return for coins, either made of gold or silver, or precious gems that were the specialty of that particular region.

NOTE: A VAISHYA COULD BE BORN IN ANY VARNA FAMILY.

4. **SHUDRAS:** The role of Shudras was typically to perform tasks assigned to them by higher varnas or individuals from those varnas, in exchange for sustenance and resources. They were commonly engaged in agricultural work, artisan crafts, and various forms of service, supporting the economic activities of society.

NOTE: A SHUDRA COULD BE BORN IN ANY VARNA FAMILY.

The resources obtained through performing one's duties (Kartavya) according to these varnas were considered part of DHARMA, which, in turn, could be used to enhance a person's Karma.

KARMA

Karma refers to the act of doing selfless deeds towards society, animals, or god's creation. it strengthens dharma and helps the soul attain Moksha while the human is still alive. Karma is further classified into three aspects:

1. Sanchit karma: The karmas that were done during a human's lifetime as a Manushya will act as a major cause

for their body, wealth, health and type of species in their present life.

2. Prarabdha karma: The reaction of karmas that are to be observed during the present life as a part of Sanchit karma.

3. Agami karma: The karmas that will be done in the future as a consequence of Prarabdha karma.

When humans sleep, their souls (Atma) depart their bodies and travel to Yam Loka, governed by Yama, the god of death, along with his assistant, Chitragupta. Chitragupta records the life data of the soul in Akasha, or space, surrounding it. So, the entirety of a human's life is stored around their body in the form of an Aura, which remains attached to the soul.

When the body dies, the atma carries the aura with itself to yam Loka, where it is used to determine the Atma's next body, whether it be a human, animal or tree, based on the karma done by the atma in its previous life.

If a human does bad Karma, such as killing innocent Beings, stealing, harming Nature or Society, the Atma triggers the subconscious mind of that person and gives him a feeling of guilt. If the person does not stop doing wrong even after feeling guilty, the atma stops alarming him, and the person falls into the slippery slope of Naraka Lokas.

The atma will continue to be in a safe zone until their Sanchit good karma is cancelled out with every bad deed they do. As the Prarabdha of the atma starts getting negative, the physical being starts facing difficulties in life and eventually a painful death.

The karma done by humans improves the aura of their bodies. While the human body feeds on food, the atma feeds on Karma. Better the Karma, healthier the Atma.

Therefore, the complete structure of human consciousness is the combination of Karma and Kartavya, which act as salvation providers or can act as a punisher. In either case, it is humans themselves who can spend a life of either a Devtas or a Daitya for which the karma will be recorded and the human will be served accordingly.

CHAPTER TWELVE

YUGAS

Manushyas (Humans) has always tried to understand the Earth's principles by comparing them with constants. In this manner, He invented the concept of time, which is just an outcome of counting the sun's position, counting the number of days, then collecting the number of days to weeks, then months, years and decades. but if we look at the whole universe, there is no concept of time. Every day, the Sun rises and every day, the sun shifts positions. Birds sing, River flows, Waterfalls and Trees grows. the basis of earth is to produce life and, in that sequence, humans try to find its existence, for that he measured the life span of every object on earth.

To understand the past and to predict the future, the Vedic Sanatan Dharma gives information about YUGAS, according to which we are living in kali yuga, that can be easily translated to dark times. Kali Yuga is believed to be the age of 4,32,000 years.

Sanatan dharma had devised yugas as a circle, which is a circle of four Yugas, i.e., Satyug, Tretayug, Dwaparyug, after that comes Kaliyug which is the last Yuga. the ages of yugas are believed to be as follows:

NAME	HUMAN YEARS	DIVINE YEARS
SATYUG	1728000	4800
TRETA YUG	1296000	3600
DWAPAR YUG	864000	2400
KALI YUG	432000	1200

These calculations of years for all the yugas are derived from the various shlokas that are derived from Mahabharata, Manu smriti and Bhagvat Geeta.

In Manu smriti (1.67) and Mahabharata (shanti parva 231.17), a shloka defines the age of divine year.

"Daive ratryahani varsham pravibhagastayo punah Ahastatrogayanam ratrih syaddakshinayanam"

One full year of Human equals to Devta's one day and night, where northern solstice is their day and southern solstice is their night. it is also mentioned in both Manu smriti and Mahabharata that 1000 divine year is equal to One night and day of brahma, after which he wakes up and creates a Mahavatar, i.e., a divine soul is born to redefine the creation.

But what is up with the calculation of years that entices humans so much? Well, it is the internal calling of all souls to get relief or moksha through the birth of Avatars. Every yuga is a combination of two properties out of four: Sharma, Arth, Kam and Moksha. At the end of every yuga, a new combination out of four arises and sets the zeitgeist of the yuga. At the end of every yuga, lord Vishnu takes the form of human and again resets the society to the Vedic functioning and returns to his Loka as said in this shloka.

"Yada Yada Hi Dharmasya Glanirva Bhavathi
Bharatha,
Abhyuthanam Adharmaysya Tadatmanam Srijami
Aham'
Praritranaya Sadhunam Vinashaya Cha
Dushkritam,
Dharamasanstha panaarthaya Sambhavami
Yuge-Yuge."

Looking at the number of years per yuga, it does not make any sense to the human mind how the earth can sustain these millions of years of human consciousness. If we equate the years of a human lifetime to hours, following the principles of Sanatan Dharma where everything is personalized, the concept of time begins to make more sense.

For example,

NAME OF YUGA	HOURS	HUMAN AVERAGE AGE YEARS
SATYUGA	1728000	197
TRETA YUGA	1296000	147
DWAPAR YUGA	864000	98
KALIYUGA	432000	49

Now, it can be easily deciphered when the average age of humans reaches the minimum as per calculation. there happens to be a war or some natural calamity that resets the Earth to its Pristine form and the new yuga begins with the establishment of Dharma by the Lord Vishnu avatar.

Every yuga possesses two of the qualities out of four, which are Dharma, Arth, Kam and Moksha, similar to how a human stands on two legs out of four limbs. at the end of every yuga, there happens a war between the incarnation of Lord Vishnu and the Daitya lord, and after the end of the war, society is reset to its basic functioning.

SAT YUGA:

In Satyuga everyone speaks the truth and there is a perfect balance between nature and humans, where people are more inclined towards attaining moksha by doing a long-time samadhi.

SATYUGA➡DHARMA X MOKSHA

In Satyug, people are more into attaining knowledge about Dharm and Practicing spiritual practices to attain moksha. It is the time when all the scriptures are written and researches are done by intense yogic practices and in this yuga, lord Vishnu takes four avatars: Matasya, Kuruma, Varah, and Narsimha to destroy the evil Daityas who try to demolish the TRIDEV by stealing the Vedic scriptures or by forcefully appointing themselves as Gods for the human race. In the end of this yuga leads to the rise of dharma and moksha for the next yuga.

TRETAYUGA:

In Tretayug the rules written in Satyuga are established. Arth and Moksha play a major role in the zeitgeist of the era.

TRETAYUGA ➡ ARTH X MOKSHA

In Tretayug, Righteousness and living by the rules are the only priorities. People are more advanced towards the creation of society and establish the laws prepared in Satyug. People start doing work according to the Varn system and gurukuls are established. Kings started creating kingdoms by arranging the resources and people for the better working of society. In this yuga, Lord Vishnu takes three avatars: Parshuram, Vamama and Shree ram.

All of these avatars work by the rule book and do the work of giving lessons to the human race. Bhagwan ram was the last avatar for this yuga and his life became the lesson for the humans (Ramayana) to understand the victory of righteousness over injustice. The end of this yuga leads to the rise of Dharma and Arth (resources) for the next yuga.

DWAPAR YUGA:

The yuga is where Kingdoms are reset, and people have started populating earth in the form of villages out of kingdoms and creating societies. Dharma and Arth play a major role in the Zeitgeist of this era.

DWAPARYUGA ➡ DHARMA X ARTH

In Dwaparyuga people led their lives according to the Dharma, yet there was infiltration of jealousy and injustice. To gather more resources, the brothers start fighting for the Arth, which made kings fight with each other for kingdoms. the dharma started declining and lord Vishnu came on earth as Balaram and Shri Krishna. Shri Krishna fought the war of dharma along with Pandavas against Kauravas without lifting a single weapon and gave cosmic knowledge to Manushyas in the form of Bhagvat Geeta. the end of this yuga gave birth to Kam and Arth for the next yuga.

KALIYUGA:

The age of darkness, the time of dusk when people forget dharma and indulge in luxuries and sensual activities and start denying the presence of God and rather try to control the other beings as well as the activities of nature. Kam and Arth play major roles in the zeitgeist of this era.

KALIYUGA ➡ KAM x ARTH

We are currently living in Kaliyuga, where the primary goal for most people is to accumulate resources and indulge in sexual activities. This has resulted in a significant increase in the human population. Unfortunately, humans are destroying the ecological system by killing animals for food and selling their skins as luxury items, which is a reflection of our foolishness. Kali is considered the main villain of this era, but he will be defeated by lord Vishnu's final avatar, Kalki avatar, after a great war. This will mark the completion of Chatur Yuga, and Satyuga will begin once again. If we look closely, no one is following dharma;

everything is being done even in Bharat as per the western ideology with a hint of Vedic culture. Many individuals perform poojas and rituals out of fear that they will incur the wrath of God if they do not do so. Yet, they then spend the rest of their day engaged in activities that harm the less fortunate, animals or the environment to earn money – a type of wealth that is considered the worst kind. This behavior is the epitome of foolishness and according to the scriptures, kali, the demon, has entered every human being, making them slaves to maya.

CHAPTER THIRTEEN

THE CONFLICT

With the birth of the Positive (Devtas), embodiments of positive energy emanating from the Trinities, came the Negative (Daityas), born to maintain equilibrium. While the Devtas crafted heavenly realms of peace, equality, tranquillity, and euphoria, the Daityas began constructing realms of pain, jealousy, suffering, and sadness. The Devtas resided in Indra Loka, while the Daityas built Nark Lokas.

Following the creation of these realms, the Devtas and Daityas began dwelling in their respective Lokas, akin to birds nesting to spend their lives. As beings of positivity, the Devtas commenced work to sustain a planet known to humans as Earth. Observing the Devtas' happiness and creation of new planets, the Daityas, embodiments of dark energy, covetously eyed the Devtas' Indra Loka. This jealousy led to continuous conflict and tension between the two factions.

Subsequently, the supreme beings convened with both sides to reach an agreement. Both entities were relocated to Bhu Loka and granted space within the bodies of humans.

This agreement entailed detailed instructions regarding human body functions, the formation of societies by the Prajapati, and the culmination of the Yuga, during which humans would engage in conflict. The Daityas were afforded a fair chance, with Bhu Loka created adjacent to Bhawar Loka and Nark Loka. Given the Daityas' insecurity and cunning, they were allotted 90% governance over Bhu Loka (Earth). Within human bodies, they were equally permitted to influence individuals with their powers, including hate, anger, jealousy, debauchery, and other unethical acts.

This information would be imparted to humans in the form of Vedas. Through these Vedas, humans would decipher various activities related to energy forms and the workings of gods. They would only gain control over these elements once the seven sages residing within the body in the form of Kundalini were activated through meditation, yoga, and karma.

Humans would establish a society affected by both Devtas and Daityas, with the victorious faction in the war at the end of the Yuga earning the right to rule the Indrasan.

Then, a detailed method of the war was created, like:

- BOTH DEVTAS AND DAITYAS WILL HAVE EQUAL POWERS TO CONTROL BHRAHMA SITTING INSIDE A HUMAN.
- NO DEVTA OR DAITYA WILL DIRECTLY GIVE MYSTICAL POWERS TO HUMAN (HUMAN WILL

HAVE TO FOLLOW RITUALS TO ATTAIN POWERS).

- A HUMAN WILL HAVE A BLANK SOUL EVERY TIME IT IS BORN ACCORDING TO THE KARMA OF HIS PREVIOUS LIFE, WHICH WILL DECIDE WHO (EITHER DEVTAS OR DAITYAS) COULD EASILY COME IN CONTACT WITH HIM.

- HUMANS WILL NOT BE ABLE TO GO TO ANY LOKA WITHOUT DYING. (OR UNTIL UNDER EXTREME ABHYASA OF MEDITATIONS, TILL HE DOES NOT AWAKEN HIS AJNA CHAKRA)

- BOTH DEVTAS AND DAAITYAS WILL HAVE 5000 YEARS OF PERIOD TO RAISE THEIR HUMAN INFLUENCE, THE END OF WHICH WAR WILL BE DECLARED.

- AT THE END OF THE WAR, THOSE WHO HAVE WON WILL ATTAIN THE SWAG LOKAS.

- THESE ENERGY BEINGS(HUMANS) WILL BE GIVEN BOOKS BY SAGES TO KNOW ABOUT THEIR BODY AND HOW TO LIVE HEALTHY LIFE.

- DAITYAS WILL ALSO PROVIDE THEM WITH BOOKS RELATED TO HOW THEY CAN ATTAIN MATERIALISTIC LUXURIES. AND THEIR OTHER PERSPECTIVES.

- DEVTAS WILL ACQUIRE ONLY 10% OF THE LAND MASS AND THE REST OF THE LAND WILL BE ACQUIRED BY DAITYAS.

- NO DAITYAS OR DANVAS ARE ALLOWED DIRECTLY TO FIGHT UNLESS WOKEN BY THE BEING.

- THE SOULS OF THE HUMAN BODY WILL BE SENT TO ATAL LOKA IF THE PERSON DIES AN UNPRECEDENT DEATH, UNLESS FREED BY THE RITUALS DONE FOR THE SOUL OR THE SOUL HAS

REACHED THE AGE OF DEATH OF THAT HUMAN BODY.

- DHARAM RAJA WILL BE APPOINTED TO THE FAIR CALCULATIONS AS PER THE KARMA DONE BY THE SOUL IN HIS /HER HUMAN FORM AND AS PER THE CALCULATIONS HE WILL GRANT EITHER SWAG LOKA OR NARAK LOKA. YET THE SOUL CAN BE GIVEN HUMAN BIRTH AGAIN AS PER THE CONDITIONS OR KARMIC BALLANCES.
- GREATER THE SINS WILL LEAD THE SOUL TO AGAIN GO THROUGH 84 LAKH YONI CYCLE TO AGAIN ATTAIN THE HUMAN BODY.

AFTER ATTAINING THE REAL KNOWLEDGE ABOUT GODS, THE ATMA WILL BE ALLOWED TO BECOME ONE WITH THE PARAMATMA.

CHAPTER FOURTEEN

4 VEDAS

The Vedas are the ancient religious scriptures that were compiled by maharishi Vyas. these ancient scriptures were originally written in Sanskrit and consisted of various mantras and hymns that laid out information about the origins of gods and their importance in life, formulas, and mantras about various rituals to be chanted while doing the offerings to gods as well as music and magical mantras to heal the human body. the whole Sanatan Dharma came out of these four Vedas, namely:

- RIG VED,
- YAJUR VED,
- SAM VED,
- ATHARVA VED.

These four Vedas are further classified into four subsections, namely: the Samihta, which consists of mantras. the brahmanas explain rituals and ceremonies to be performed, while yajnas/yagyas. the Aranyaka talks about symbolic meta-realistic points of view about rituals, and the Upanishads talk about philosophy, spiritual knowledge and how to do meditation.

Further, 3 major story books speak about the glory of gods and give a basic understanding to humans of how Lord Vishnu took the human form and defeated the asuras (Daityas). these books are Ramayana, Bhagwat Geeta and Mahabharata, where Ramayana tells the story of lord ram defeating the wrongdoer rakshasa named Ravan, Mahabharat tells the tale of five brothers fighting a hundred brothers for righteousness and in between the battlefield Shri Krishna gave the knowledge about this world and all the aspect of Dharma to Arjun, to give him courage and direction while fighting with his blood brothers.

CHAPTER FIFTEEN

FOOD

There exist three types of Gun (CHARACTERISTICS) in every human body namely

- RAJOGUN
- TAMOGUN
- SATAVGUN

RAJOGUN: The functioning of a body undergoing excessive labor is influenced by the concept of "rajogun" in Hindu philosophy. Rajogun is associated with activity, passion, and restlessness. Foods classified as "Rajsik" are believed to provide energy necessary for such activities, typically being rich in calories. However, an imbalance in rajogun may lead to a heightened pursuit of materialistic gains and constant striving for bodily pleasures. This excessive pursuit can sometimes drive individuals to engage in unethical or criminal activities as they become disconnected from their sense of humanity. Rajsik foods often include spicy and stimulating ingredients, which, when consumed excessively, can be detrimental to physical and mental health.

TAMOGUN: "Tamogun" represents inertia, darkness, and lethargy. It's considered essential for rest and sleep, crucial for the body's rejuvenation. However, foods that induce continuous laziness and lethargy are discouraged in Vedic Sanatan Dharma, as they hinder productivity and purposeful living. A person dominated by Tamogun tends to avoid work and may lead a purposeless life. Furthermore, such tendencies can incline individuals towards easier but unethical paths, such as relying on animal products rather than engaging in the toil of growing crops and vegetables. Tamsik foods typically include meat and pungent spices like garlic. Overindulgence in such foods can lead to a state of dullness and sluggishness, both physically and mentally, hindering personal growth and spiritual development.

SATOGUN: The ideal state for a human being is believed to be a balance between "Rajogun" and "Tamogun". When an individual possesses this balance, they are well-equipped to lead a constructive life, effectively channelling their energy. Optimal nutrition for the human body is found in foods rich in essential vitamins, minerals, and proteins, while being low in both Rajsik and Tamsik qualities. Such foods promote efficient bodily functions without causing harm to internal organs or disturbing internal peace.

According to the principles of Ayurveda, this balanced diet is akin to consuming food as medicine. Herbs and spices used in daily meals help maintain the equilibrium of gunas, resulting in a Satvik diet.

Individuals who consume predominantly Tamsik foods are believed to be more susceptible to negative influences, potentially leading them to engage in destructive behaviour. Therefore, understanding the importance of food intake is crucial for one's interactions with deities and gods.

Consuming a Satvik diet is thought to facilitate a closer connection to the divine ("Paramatma" or "Bhagwan"), making it easier to receive divine guidance and solutions to life's challenges. Increasing Satvik qualities can foster spiritual growth, eventually leading to the ability to sustain bodily functions for extended periods without food, known as "Samadhi." Attaining Samadhi allows individuals to enter a meditative state, transcending earthly concerns and ultimately leading to liberation ("moksha"). This journey also involves acquiring knowledge about the divine through contact with Gods during Samadhi experiences.

CHAPTER SIXTEEN

PURANAS

18 PURANAS consist of stories and hymns related to specific deities, which talk about various rituals and aspects of life and how to deal with different problems of life. The names of these Puranas are:

Brahma Purana, Padma Purana, Vishnu Purana, Shiva Purana, Bhagvat Purana, Narad purana, Agni Purana, Markandeya Purana, Bhavishya Purana, Brahmavaivarvit Purana, Linga Purana, Varah Purana, Skand Purana, Vamana Purana, Kuruma Puran, Matasya Puran, Garud Puran, Brahmand Puran.

SHASTRAS: There are various SHASTRAS that provide knowledge about specific fields of knowledge. These shastras consist of SUTRAS to be performed in daily life as a part of DHARMA. The names of these SHASTRAS are:

YOG VASHISHTHA, ALAMKARA SHASTRA, VASTU SHASTRA, VAIMANIKA SHASTRA, DHARMA SHASTRA, KAMA SHASTRA, ARTH SHASTRA, MOKSHOPAYA, NATYA SHASTRA, SURYA SIDHANTA, SAMUDRIKA SHASTRA, SHILPA SHASTRA, NAYAYA

SHASTRA, KAVYA SHASTRA, RASA SHASTRA.

These Shastras talk about various artistic knowledge respectively:

1. YOG VASHISHTHA: Gives knowledge about YOGA
2. ALAMKARA SHASTRA: Gives knowledge about LANGUAGE
3. VASTU SHASTRA: Gives Knowledge about ARCHITECTURE
4. VAIMANIKA SHASTRA: Gives knowledge about AERONAUTICS
5. DHARMA SHASTRA: Gives knowledge about DHARMIC RITUALS and DUTIES
6. KAMA SHASTRA: GIVES knowledge about SEXUAL DESIRES and EMOTIONAL LONGINGS
7. ARTH SHASTRA: Gives knowledge about ATTAINING WEALTH WHILE STAYING IN LIMITS OF DHARMA
8. MOKSHOPAYA: Talks about how to attain NIRVANA
9. NATYA SHASTRA: Gives knowledge about DANCE
10. SURYA SIDHANTA: Gives knowledge about ASTRONOMY
11. SAMUDRIKA SHASTRA: Gives knowledge about EFFECTS OF PLANETS ON HUMAN BEING
12. SHILPA SHASTRA: Gives knowledge about PAINTING, CARPENTRY, METALURGY and SCULPTURES
13. NAYAYA SHASTRA: Gives knowledge about providing legal judgements for social issues
14. KAVYA SHASTRA: Gives knowledge about POETICS
15. RASA SHASTRA: Gives knowledge about AYURVEDA and various EFFECTS OF ELEMENTS on HUMAN.

These are the various subjects in the form of shastras, Vedas, and puranas that were taught in gurukuls along with the art of fighting war, known as Shustra vidya. ancient Bharat was technically advanced, and it was doing continuous experiments that were stolen from Bharat and copyrighted by many modern-day scientists.

Even after getting looted and getting its knowledge bank burned to ashes, Bharat still holds the essence of Bhagwan, but the real meaning to it got lost.

CHAPTER SEVENTEEN

CONCLUSION

It can be interpreted that the human body contains representations of various realms or Lokas, through which the soul or Atma travels during its lifetime. According to this perspective, when a person experiences happiness, the soul ascends to higher Lokas, whereas during times of distress, it descends to lower Lokas. Within the body, the entities symbolizing creation, sustenance, and procreation, represented as Brahma, Vishnu, and Mahesh, respectively, perform their functions. Meanwhile, the Atma, as a projection of the divine or Paramatma, serves to awaken individuals to their consciousness and guide them towards awareness of their actions or Karma. This interpretation sheds light on the deeper meaning of the phrase

"YAT PINDE TAT BRAHMANDE"

"ALL THAT IS OUTSIDE YOU IS WITHIN YOU"

"Much like how an apple tree absorbs nutrients from the soil and transforms them into fruits bearing no resemblance to the soil's taste, humans undergo a similar transformation. We are nature's most exquisite creation, crafted from the five elemental building blocks, yet we do not manifest the essence of those elements in our taste. In essence, all living beings are composed of the same fundamental matter. However, humans hold a distinctive position, as nature has endowed us with the capacity to serve as the cognitive center for the environment we inhabit."

As the Earth trembles under the looming shadow of an impending war between Devtas and Daityas, more and more humans are succumbing to the influence of these opposing energies. The planet quakes with the bloodshed of peace-loving creatures caught in the crossfire. Amidst this cosmic battle, each individual's soul is a battleground, influenced by the forces of good and evil. Every action we take, whether it be good or bad karma, reflects the ongoing struggle between these divine and demonic influences, shaping the destiny of our Atma.

We as the human race, have lost the essence of being a creature that were designed by GODS to maintain his creation and opposite to that, we have destroyed every environment we touched. We are killing animals for the sake of our TASTE, not for our body and we are cutting trees for the sake of having LUXURIES. We are displacing animals for the sake of LAND to build nature-harming HOMES and FACTORIES. We are growing in population just like RAKTHBEEJ (A demon that grew in more numbers with his blood splash on Earth). All of the activities only suggest one thing (We Do NOT BELONG TO EARTH) If we did belong here, we would not have created HAVOC on this pristine planet because if I ask you to go and burn down your home, you will never do it at any cost.

But what went wrong? Why are humans behaving this way? Why are only humans being SELFISH? Well, if you have read all of the chapters of this book, you would have understood the cause and effects of every Good Deed and every Bad Effect. There is a story about Deamon KALI where he talks with LORD VISHNU that I will not be a fool anymore like in my previous births where I took the physical forms and got killed by you in every YUGA, In Kali yuga I will enter in the bodies of all the humans whether spiritual or not, and if you have to defeat me, you will have to kill all your DEVOTEES first. The demon Kali's influence has spread to every human, regardless of their devotion to God. He controls the minds of people in this era, transforming them into deceptive figures—white-clad devils—difficult to distinguish from God's beloved children.

Now, if we look at today's scenario, people who talk about nature or try to live a modest life are ridiculed by society, and people who bark like dogs are considered PANDITS. Societies have crumbled into a system that only serves as a machine that produces mass LABOURERS. An army of frustrated and self-loathing humans who work their lifetime aimlessly and, in the end, they are left with no peace or harmony inside.

"THERE WAS A TIME WHEN PEOPLE USED
TO DIE AND SOULS WANDERED.
BUT TODAY, IT SEEMS LIKE SOULS HAVE
DIED AND PEOPLE ARE WANDERING."

When a society is full of honest people, they help the wrongdoer to a righteous path and when a society is full of immoral people, they mold the religion as per their requirement where they are not pinpointed for something wrong, they are doing.

Looking at today's Bharat, anyone with 1 percent knowledge of Vedic dharma can decipher that no one follows Vedas. People are finding ways to blend Dharma at their own ease. Opposite to that, DHARMA is purely a way to lead a sustainable yet purposeful life where people do not harm Mother Earth and in return, she grants them good health and peace of mind. Name any activity from day to night we have adopted the Daitya's ways.

From Education to daily chores, no Dharma teachings are followed. We are doing things according to Religions with a hint of Vedic Sanskrit. We have no respect for our Vedas, and we have all seen videos saying that our Shastras teachings have been approved by scientists. This is what I call an inferiority complex. This statement clearly shows that people are not taking Vedas and Shastras seriously and are depending on some goons to approve what our rishis and Tapsvis did thousands of years back in time and gave us these wonderful guidebooks viz. VEDAS, UPNISHADS, RAMAYANA, BHAVAD GEETA, MAHABHART, and MANY TANTRAS to check if we are on the right path. Contrary to that, people are reciting the Verses of Ramayana or Geeta.

So that they can fluently speak those Verses and look religious PANDITS in front of other people, this only boost their ego and, in the end, this ego eat away their purity.

No one is trying to learn real lessons from RAMAYANA, which can easily be translated into simple words if the elder brother becomes RAMA and his wife behaves like SEETA. If a younger brother behaves like LAKSHMAN, BHARAT, OR SHATRUGHAN. If a devotee becomes like Veer HANUMAN. Then Ram Rajya has already established in a society where no one had to bring RAMA or call for him.

GEETA is there as a reference to check when a person is on Adhyatam Way. He will automatically learn the teachings of Geeta from his soul. No one has to recite the teachings. It comes without reading, and if you are not sure whether you are getting the right message from your soul, you can check the Geeta and your Atamgyan will match.

In Garud Puran, Lord Vishnu also mentions the same thing: I am not pleased with the Poojas, Alters or any rituals that you do for me. I am very happy to provide NIRVANA to a person who tries to attain ATAMGYAN.

There is a story about Brahma and Maya. When Brahma created the universe, he created planet Earth and different animals to sustain it. Then, Maya came to Brahma and said great work, but it seems MECHANICAL, as there are 100 deer and 20 lions to eat them and different animals are all Mechanically doing the work. It seems boring. Then Brahma asked what we should do then. Maya said make a creature who looks like PARAMATMA but with two hands and two legs and all other necessary organs and then I will cut you (BRAHMA) into pieces and put you into every one of those creatures and sitting in those bodies, you try to find your origins and I will play the work of distraction.

The day you will find God sitting in that body, that soul will be liberated from the cycle of birth and death. By now, you have known every aspect of how you are the embodiment of GOD himself. That is why TAT TVAM ASI is written on every page of this book. It is you that is going to change the world inside you. It is you who is creating Brahm inside you, and it is you who is going to come out of that Brahm.

If Kali is sitting in every Human, then this Knowledge is going to awaken the KALKI sitting in each one of you. Those who have read this book have read about every aspect of being a Human first and can easily decipher what Karmas are, what Kartavya is and how you can be useful for the Gods just by being a Human that is awakened to his senses and not harming animals or not trying to impose his superiority on fellow beings, just by trying to live a life that is full of good intentions towards other beings and plants and reducing your load on Mother Earth and sustainably using the natural resources and keeping God in mind while doing any deed.

It can be easily understood that we are responsible for what happens in our environment. No God will directly intervene in our lives unless our Karma is pure. Our body is embodiment of Gods and our Atma feeds on our Karmas. Good karmas will elevate our Atma to upper Lokas, and we will stand among Devtas. Bad karmas will make us stand among Daityas. In both cases, we will meet God in the end, but the outcome will be different. Standing among Devtas, we will attain moksha and standing among Daityas, we will face the wrath of Gods.

This work will make you understand the concept of gods and will make you decipher the real meaning of the phrase AHAM BRAHMASMI. After this knowledge, a person can start deciphering the mysterious Gyan written about Tattvas and how to control them to reach the realms of Devtas and can easily defeat Daityas. But misuse of this knowledge will put a curse on the whole life and family of that person leading to miseries and mis happenings.

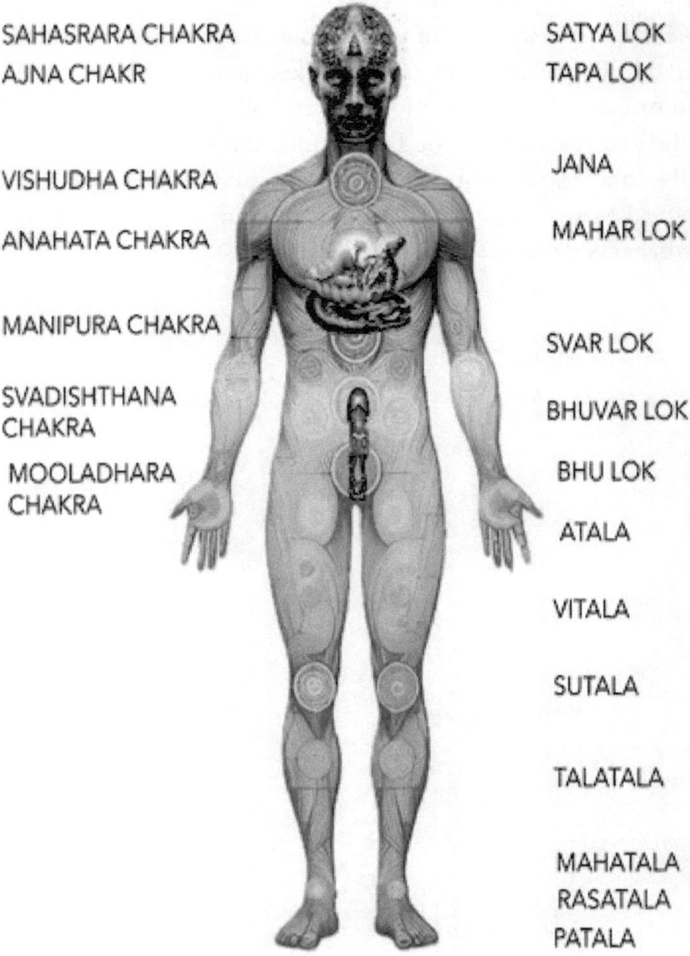

SAHASRARA CHAKRA
AJNA CHAKR
VISHUDHA CHAKRA
ANAHATA CHAKRA
MANIPURA CHAKRA
SVADISHTHANA
CHAKRA
MOOLADHARA
CHAKRA
SATYA LOK
TAPA LOK
JANA
MAHAR LOK
SVAR LOK
BHUVAR LOK
BHU LOK
ATALA
VITALA
SUTALA
TALATALA
MAHATALA
RASATALA
PATALA

I, NITISH SHARMA (MANU) S/O KAMLESH KUMARI and KAMAL KUMAR SHARMA, am putting forth my ATAMGYAN in front of you as this was given to me by my GURU Lord Shiva. He gave me the chance and allowed me to present this information, which will help you get out of illusion. It will help you live a more serene and purposeful life and will make you understand the SANATAN DHARMA. This enables you to help your children decipher what reality is and what imagination is.

HARI OM TAT SAT

GLOSSARY

1. BHAGWAN - GOD
2. DEVTA - DEITY
3. DAITYA - DEAMON
4. ASURA - DEAMON
5. MANUSHYA - HUMAN
6. ATMA - SOUL
7. PARAMATMA - SUPREME SOUL
8. BHARAT -INDIA
9. MOKSHA -NIRVANA
10. ARTH - RESOURCES
11. YUGA - ERA
12. SHASTRA - BOOK ON A PARTICULAR SUBJECT
13. SHUSTRA - WEAPON
14. LOKA -REALM
15. MRUTYU- DEATH

NOTES

NOTES

NOTES